JESUS CHRIST
THE ULTIMATE SOCIAL WORKER

A 31-Day Devotional
for Social Workers

JUNE TYSON PH.D & LCSW

ISBN 978-1-0980-2627-1 (paperback)
ISBN 978-1-0980-2628-8 (digital)

Christian Faith Publishing, Inc.
832 Park Avenue
Meadville, PA 16335
www.christianfaithpublishing.com

Printed in the United States of America

DAY 1

❦

Bringing Light and Peace:
The Goal of Social Work

Read Luke 1.

Focus: Luke 1:78-79

Luke 1 paints a beautiful picture of important events leading up to Jesus' birth. God carefully prepared people for Christ's coming by demonstrating miraculous signs to prove the seriousness of His plans. Zechariah prophesied that Jesus, the Light of the World, was to shine upon a planet in darkness and guide it to peace.

This is the essence of social work—the Lord bringing many people to us for light and peace, for this is the ultimate goal of our work. God will use us in many ways in order to achieve this goal, and we must be ready to be used.

List three ways you can prepare yourself now to let your light shine and guide your clients to peace.

_____

_____

_____

_____

_____

_____

_____

_____

_____

_____

_____

_____

_____

Write a brief prayer asking the Lord to assist you in your preparation.

_____

_____

_____

_____

_____

_____

_____

_____

_____

_____

_____

_____

_____

_____

DAY 2

Social Work is God's Work

Read Luke 2.

Focus: Luke 2:49

In the verses above, Jesus does not waste a moment's time. He begins His duties as a social worker at a very young age, expounding on the Scriptures with men in the temple, with great power and authority, and those around Him are very impressed.

His parents, however, are not initially impressed, because they have been frantically looking for Him. But Jesus informs His parents that they should have known He was doing His Father's work. This should be our reputation in the social work field. Everyone should know us as people who are about the great work of our clients' healing and peace, because social work is God's work.

Prayerfully consider Jesus' words to His parents. Think about how focused He was on His obligation as a social worker. He understood the work He was doing was God's work. Now describe your own attitude as a social worker.

_____

_____

_____

_____

_____

_____

_____

_____

_____

_____

_____

_____

_____

Construct a prayer asking God to show you ways your mind-set can become more like Jesus' as He conducted His work as a social worker.

_____

_____

_____

_____

_____

_____

_____

_____

_____

_____

_____

_____

DAY 3

Social Work is a Calling

Read Luke 3.

Focus: Luke 3:21-22

Social work is a calling. One must be sure that God has put this work in his/her heart to do for His glory. Because the work can be emotionally demanding and trying, much prayer and Bible study are required. In verses 21 and 22, Jesus is called to do the great and holy work before Him. God confirmed this to us as He made His support and validation known to all who were present at Jesus' baptism. After this event, Jesus began His earthy ministry as the ultimate social worker.

Have you been called to be a social worker? How can you be sure of this? List three ways in which God has confirmed this calling to your heart.

_____

_____

_____

_____

_____

_____

_____

_____

_____

_____

_____

_____

_____

Compose a prayer asking God to make this fact clear to you if you are unsure. If you are sure, create a brief prayer of thanksgiving and rejoicing, knowing you are in God's purpose for your life.

_____

_____

_____

_____

_____

_____

_____

_____

_____

_____

_____

_____

DAY 4

A Method of Grace: Responding to the Challenges of Social Work

Read Luke 4.

Focus: Luke 4:1-13

Social work can be very political. You may find yourself being tempted to do things that go against the purpose of your work, your character, and your Christian sensibilities. Jesus found Himself in such a predicament; however, notice the graceful way in which He conducted Himself. He did not become unruly, loud, or inappropriate in any way. Instead, He used the Scriptures to combat Satan's tactics. You will discover this method of grace will be very useful in the social work field or in any other capacity in which God places you.

When was the last time Satan confronted you with a challenge? Describe your response.

_____

_____

_____

_____

_____

_____

_____

_____

_____

List three ways in which you could have responded more like Jesus, using His method of grace, in the above verses.

_____

_____

_____

_____

_____

_____

_____

_____

_____

Write a prayer asking God to help you respond to personal and professional trials by using His Word.

_____

_____

_____

_____

_____

_____

_____

_____

Day 5

Social Work and Personal Devotion Time: A Balancing Act

Read Luke 5.

Focus: Luke 5:1-16

At this point in Jesus' work as the ultimate social worker, He has established a huge following. People want to experience the wisdom of His teachings and the power of His healing. Jesus accommodated His followers by giving them what they needed, which caused Him to be very busy and preoccupied. He did not neglect His spiritual life, however. In fact, verse 16 states that He would withdraw alone to pray as often as possible. So instead of allowing this work to interfere with His connection to God, He delicately balanced His duties as a social worker with His relationship with His Father. This is an important and necessary practice for all social workers.

With an open heart, examine the time you take to be alone with God. Is it quality time? Is it enough time? Do you even make time?

_____

_____

_____

_____

_____

_____

_____

_____

_____

_____

_____

Now compose a prayer. Pray that the time you spend with God becomes a more enhanced and beautiful experience, and that it is done as often as possible. For it is our relationship with the Lord that will make us as social workers great and effective.

_____

_____

_____

_____

_____

_____

_____

_____

_____

_____

_____

DAY 6

The Power of Open-Ended Questions

Read Luke 6.

Focus: Luke 6:1-11

As in many professions, the social work field has a code of ethics, which has been established primarily to ensure ethical services for the benefit of the clients. We prayerfully serve our clients with these practices in our hearts and minds.

As Jesus performed His responsibilities as the ultimate social worker, He was expected to follow the code of ethics of His day, the s and customs of the Jews. Today's reading shows Jesus breaking one of the elements of the Law. In doing so, He asks His critics an open-ended question: "Is it better to help or hurt your fellow man on the Sabbath?" Open-ended questions require a great deal of thought and more than a simple one-word answer. Jesus made His critics and His followers think deeply about the root of the issue, helping someone in need.

Is the Lord leading you to ask your clients open-ended questions? Do you ask them well? Write a time where you were able to get a client to think deeply about something.

_____

_____

_____

_____

_____

_____

_____

_____

_____

_____

_____

_____

_____

Compose a prayer asking God to lead you to ask your clients wise and thought-provoking open-ended questions.

_____

_____

_____

_____

_____

_____

_____

_____

_____

_____

_____

_____

_____

_____

DAY 7

※※※

Using Supervision Creatively

Read Luke 6.

Focus: Luke 6:12-16

These verses show how important prayer was to Jesus' earthly ministry. We see Him praying before deciding whom He would choose as His twelve apostles. He knew these men would be the future leaders of His early church, so this was not a light decision. So, as the Word says, He went to a mountain and prayed all night before choosing the apostles.

As social workers, we also have major decisions that will take wisdom and insight to make. We want our decisions to glorify God and be the best decisions we can make for our clients. At times, we will need the guidance of our supervisors, but at all times, we must inquire of God before making a choice. The assistance of our supervisors, plus direction from God during prayer, will be most effective in making wise decisions concerning our clients.

Write a brief prayer asking God to make you more conscientious in your prayer life regarding your profession. Ask for His creative supervision to assist you in your work with your clients.

_____
_____
_____
_____
_____
_____
_____
_____
_____
_____
_____
_____
_____
_____
_____
_____
_____
_____
_____
_____
_____
_____
_____
_____
_____
_____
_____
_____
_____
_____
_____
_____

DAY 8

Human Services Require the "Human Touch"

Read Luke 7.

Focus: Luke 7:11-15

Social workers often find themselves overwhelmed with meeting deadlines, billing, paperwork, and many other responsibilities. During such times, we can lose our "human touch." We may rush a client out of our office because we have a meeting. Or we may not show empathy to one of our clients because of the number of others who are waiting in the reception area to see us. This is common and quite natural. We are human beings after all. Nevertheless, we will never be as busy as Jesus was during His earthly ministry.

In the above verses, we see Jesus' heart overflowing with compassion for a widow who lost her son. By showing compassion, He connected to this woman in a way that prompted Him to work a great miracle for her. Likewise, God uses our compassion to help our clients in very special ways. So, we must not lose the "human touch" in our work. We must make the time to show compassion and other characteristics that will connect us with our clients.

Prayerfully evaluate the way you deal with your clients. How do you feel about their struggles and challenges? How does the Lord use these feelings to impact your work for your clients?

_____

_____

_____

_____

_____

_____

_____

_____

_____

_____

_____

_____

_____

_____

Write a prayer asking the Lord to help you remain sensitive to your clients' situations regardless of how busy or overwhelmed you are.

_____

_____

_____

_____

_____

_____

_____

_____

_____

_____

_____

_____

_____

DAY 9

There is No Room for Favoritism in Social Work

Read Luke 8.

Focus: Luke 8:19-21

As social workers, we have a huge caseload filled with clients, some of whom you may prefer to help and others you may not prefer to help. This is only natural. The desire to help the ones you favor, however, may outweigh the desire to help the others. But there is no room for favoritism in the social work field. We must give all our clients the best of ourselves.

In the above verses, we see characteristics that may seem cold-hearted and unkind to some. Jesus did not give His mother and brothers any preferential treatment because of kinship. As the ultimate social worker, He understood those who needed help were His priority.

Reflect on the way you treat the clients you favor. Compare your responses to them with the way you respond to the clients you do not favor. Write a prayer asking God to help you balance the treatment of your clients so that all of them receive the best of your loving heart, talents, and skills.

_____
_____
_____
_____
_____
_____
_____
_____
_____
_____
_____
_____
_____
_____
_____
_____
_____
_____
_____
_____
_____
_____
_____
_____
_____
_____
_____
_____

DAY 10

Empowerment: The Beauty of Independence

Read Luke 9.

Focus: Luke 9:1-6

The goal of social work is not only to assist our clients with the necessities of life, but also to empower them to become independent. We are to give them the tools to live autonomously, and ultimately, without the constant need for social services. We do not want our clients to live on public assistance if they have the strength to work for a living. Assisting them when they have met with financial difficulties is our job. We should also be grooming them, however, for a time when they can live and function productively on their own.

We see Jesus doing this with His apostles in the above verses. First, He gave them the power to cast out demons, heal the sick, and preach the Gospel. Then, He sent them out on their own to do the work. This is how we must work with our clients. We must give them the power to live freely and in the beauty of independence.

Examine the way you work with your clients. Are you empowering them to one day live without the services you provide? If so, how? If not, why?

_____

_____

_____

_____

_____

_____

_____

_____

_____

_____

_____

_____

_____

What are some creative ways in which the Lord can use you to empower you clients to live in the beauty of independence?

_____

_____

_____

_____

_____

_____

_____

_____

_____

_____

_____

_____

_____

DAY 11

Accepting Rejection

Read Luke 10.

Focus: Luke 10:1-24

In today's reading, we see Jesus sending out seventy-two disciples without Him. Before He sends them out, however, He instructs them, encourages them, warns them what to expect, and tells them what they should do if someone rejects the Gospel. He also tells them to warn these people of their coming fate.

As we know, not all our clients will accept the help we as social workers offer them. They may reject the requirements for our service. Perhaps they may reject certain elements of the treatment plan designed to address their issues.

It is very easy to take this rejection personally, as if our clients were rejecting us. We must learn, however, to accept rejection by understanding the root of the situation. As Jesus stated, they are not rejecting us; they are rejecting Jesus and all He has to give them. We must, therefore, gracefully accept the rejection and prayerfully warn our clients of the consequences of their choices.

Recall a time when a client rejected one of the services you wanted to provide for them. What was your reaction? Did you take it personally?

_____
_____
_____
_____
_____
_____
_____
_____
_____
_____
_____
_____
_____

Now that you have read today's Scriptures, how could you have reacted better to that same situation? Keep in mind what you have learned from Jesus' words on how to accept rejection.

_____
_____
_____
_____
_____
_____
_____
_____
_____
_____
_____
_____
_____
_____

DAY 12

The Importance of Being Consistent

Read Luke 11.

Focus: Luke 11:1-13

The Lord has shown us the importance of empowering our clients. In today's reading, He continues to enhance our knowledge in this skill. We see Jesus empowering His disciples not only in teaching them to pray, but also in teaching them to be consistent in their prayer lives.

Consistency is one of the most essential steps to being truly empowered. There must be a commitment to consistency because there will be too many times when giving up is the more appealing and easier option. As social workers, we must stress the importance of being consistent, as Jesus did in the above verses.

Frustration, impatience, and aggravation will make our clients want to give up and walk away from any progress made because their needs and desires take a long time to come to fruition. Teaching them the importance of being consistent, however, will help give them the fortitude they need to endure.

What creative ways has the Lord given you to help your clients be more consistent?

_____
_____
_____
_____
_____
_____
_____
_____
_____
_____
_____
_____
_____
_____
_____
_____
_____
_____
_____
_____
_____
_____
_____
_____
_____
_____
_____
_____
_____

DAY 13

❧

The Art of Prioritizing: A Required Skill in Social Work

Read Luke 12.

Focus: Luke 12:13-21

Our clients will come to us with a myriad of housing, relational, and financial challenges, just to name a few. Because our clients will be overwhelmed with their challenges, they may not know how to address the most important issues first. This is where we as social workers can assist them.

In our profession, we must know how to prioritize. We see Jesus, the ultimate social worker, demonstrating this skill in the above verses. Instead of addressing the lesser issue of money, for example, He addresses the more important issue of the soul. By skillfully using the art of prioritizing, therefore, Jesus shifted the focus from the less important things to the one thing needed in one's life.

How anointed and skillful are you at prioritizing? Think of your most challenging client. In what ways can you refine your prioritization skills for the glory of God and the edification of this client in particular?

_____
_____
_____
_____
_____
_____
_____
_____
_____
_____
_____
_____
_____
_____
_____
_____
_____
_____
_____
_____
_____
_____
_____
_____
_____
_____
_____
_____

DAY 14

The Keen Observation
of a Social Worker

Read Luke 13.

Focus: 13:10-17

Again, in the above verses, we see Jesus healing on the Sabbath. As He is teaching, He sees a woman who has been crippled by an evil spirit. He sees her illness, its origin, and the length of time she has suffered, and He heals her. Notice that Jesus is observing His audience even as He is teaching them. He sees their problems and takes time to address their challenges.

In our role as social workers, we too must be able to see the true issues of our clients to assist them properly. To accomplish this, we must be able to communicate with and listen to our clients. If we do not take the time required to observe our clients in a deep and thorough manner, we may overlook the most important needs they have.

In our field, it is important to bill our clients, write progress notes, and execute treatment plans, among other things. As a result, we can become overwhelmed and too busy to observe our clients' deepest needs. In the space below, write a heartfelt prayer asking the Lord to help you take the time to look into your clients' hearts and see the true and secret needs that even they may not be aware of.

_____
_____
_____
_____
_____
_____
_____
_____
_____
_____
_____
_____
_____
_____
_____
_____
_____
_____
_____
_____
_____
_____
_____
_____
_____

DAY 15

Firmness and Gentleness: A Balancing Act

Read Luke 13.

Focus: Luke 13:31-35

In today's reading, we see the firmness and gentleness of Jesus manifested in a short but meaningful discourse as He addresses Jerusalem's behavior, past and present. He grieves deeply for the city, describing how He wanted to comfort and protect it.

We will find ourselves in similar situations with our clients. As social workers, we will need to confront our clients about their behaviors and actions that may be hindering their progress as we console, edify, and encourage them.

The delicate balance of firmness and gentleness requires a great deal of prayer in order to nurture them so that we are able to give our clients quality services.

How well do you balance firmness and gentleness when working with your clients? How can you become more balanced? Write a short prayer asking God to assist you in those ways.

_____
_____
_____
_____
_____
_____
_____
_____
_____
_____
_____
_____
_____
_____
_____
_____
_____
_____
_____
_____
_____
_____
_____
_____
_____
_____
_____
_____
_____
_____

DAY 16

Fortitude is a Must in Social Work

Read Luke 14.

Focus Luke 14:1-6

If you have not experienced opposition as a social worker, you will. It is a very bureaucratic and political field. As we advocate for our clients, we may find those who are unwilling to work with us due to a lack of money, time, or resources; however, we must develop the fortitude to work around and pray for such people for the good of our clients.

In the above Scriptures, once again, Jesus heals a sick man on the Sabbath while they are both at the home of a Pharisee leader. Although we see Jesus constantly in opposition with the leaders of the Jewish people, He is consistent in being the ultimate social worker as He advocates for the sick, heals them, teaches them, and loves them. This takes fortitude, which is a must for those who want to be social workers who will make a difference in the lives of their clients.

Examine your heart. Do you have the fortitude needed to be a strong social worker in the face of opposition? Do you have the desire to possess this attribute? List 5 inspired ways you can obtain it. Write a prayer asking God to assist you in obtaining this characteristic for His glory.

_____

_____

_____

_____

_____

_____

_____

_____

_____

_____

_____

_____

_____

_____

_____

_____

_____

_____

_____

_____

_____

_____

_____

_____

_____

_____

_____

_____

DAY 17

Desiring the Undesirable: The Heart of Social Work

Read Luke 15.

Focus Luke 15:1-2

We are aware that our duties as social workers will require us to work with what the world calls "the undesirables." This, however, is the heart of social work, desiring those who are undesirable. These are the very people to whom God calls us to show the beauty of His grace.

Jesus was very comfortable associating with this population. In today's reading, we see that He even visited their homes. Jesus did not treat them any different from the other people He assisted. As social workers, we too will need to make these people feel as if they are no different from anyone else because this is how God sees them.

Which population in the social work field do you feel the least comfortable with? Is it the homeless? Is it the sex offenders? Perhaps it is the drug addicts. Consider why you are uncomfortable with this population. Write a prayer asking God to help you remove these apprehensions and see them as He does so you can provide them with useful services.

DAY 18

Using Illustrations to "Bring the Point Home" to Our Clients

Read Luke 15.

Focus: Luke 15:3

Notice how Jesus freely used beautiful illustrations to make various points. He did so with great skill, which made His stories very vivid and comprehensible. Observe how useful they are not only in describing the heart of man, but also in giving us a glimpse into the heart of God.

In our social work, we may need to use creative means to illustrate healthy thinking and living. Using various tools regularly such as roleplaying and storytelling, even using biblical stories, to "bring a point home" can be very effective throughout our careers.

How can you enhance your storytelling skills to show your clients different sides of a situation? Write a prayer asking God to assist you in enriching your storytelling techniques.

_____
_____
_____
_____
_____
_____
_____
_____
_____
_____
_____
_____
_____
_____
_____
_____
_____
_____
_____
_____
_____
_____
_____
_____
_____
_____
_____
_____

DAY 19

✦

Being Resourceful

Read Luke 16.

Focus: Luke 16:1-13

In today's reading, Jesus tells His disciples the story of the "Shrewd Manager." He not only teaches them about the importance of being resourceful, astute, and ingenious, but He also teaches them to be faithful, loyal, and responsible. They will need these attributes when they begin building the church.

We need these same attributes to work effectively with our clients, who will come from various populations. To be resourceful, we need to be able to find "loopholes," exceptions to various rules, as well as hidden funds and other assets. We may even be called to advocate for our clients. If so, we need to be able to creatively present their cases while maintaining our commitment to the code of ethics, the law, and our Lord Jesus Christ.

Are you aware of the various resources available to your clients? How savvy are you in using them? How is God leading you to develop the attributes discussed in order to assist your clients more thoroughly?

DAY 20

The Willingness to Warn

Read Luke 17.

Focus: Luke 17:1-4

A social worker's tasks can be disturbing and difficult. One of the difficult tasks we must do is warn our clients when needed. This is our responsibility and one of our Christian duties.

You may notice a client's behavior is unwise or dangerous. Continual drug use, fornication, adultery, and stealing are behaviors that are frequently seen in social work, and God expects us to warn our clients of the consequences of such actions. In doing so, we help prevent them from going down a path they will regret.

In the above passage, we see Jesus warning His disciples of the consequences of questionable behavior and using some vivid and frightening language to describe the penalties of these actions. Likewise, we must possess the willingness to warn our clients of the costs of their conduct when it is perilous.

How willing are you to have these conversations with your clients if they are engaging in risky behavior? If you do not have the willingness to warn, why? Comprise a prayer asking God to move past your unwillingness to warn your clients when required. Ask Him for the words to say to your clients to describe the consequences of their actions if they persist.

_____

_____

_____

_____

_____

_____

_____

_____

_____

_____

_____

_____

_____

_____

_____

_____

_____

_____

_____

_____

_____

_____

_____

_____

_____

_____

_____

_____

_____

DAY 21

Encouraging Persistence in Our Clients

Read Luke 18.

Focus: Luke 18:1-8

It is difficult for anyone to endure trials with patience. Given the positions our clients find themselves in, it may be more difficult for them to practice this virtue. This is why we must be understanding when our clients exhibit a lack of patience with the treatment process and want to give up. We must also, however, encourage them to be persistent in their efforts toward a better life.

Today's reading teaches the reward of being persistent. Many of our clients' present conditions did not manifest themselves overnight. It took years for them to find themselves in their situations, and it may take years for their conditions to change. Nevertheless, if they are persistent and constant in the pursuit of their goals, they will discover the beauty from the results of their efforts.

As social workers, we must encourage our clients to be persistent. We can see the fruit of this characteristic very clearly, just as Jesus did. Our job is to encourage the faith and consistency needed for our clients to make their desires for a better life a reality.

Do you ever want to give up on a client who continues to make poor and unhealthy choices? This is a very natural response; however, we must model the persistency that we teach them and continue to encourage and pray for those clients who do not make quick progress. Compose a prayer for those clients who require more of your encouragement to be persistent in their goals. Pray that you continue to motivate them to be persistent.

_____

_____

_____

_____

_____

_____

_____

_____

_____

_____

_____

_____

_____

_____

_____

_____

_____

_____

_____

_____

_____

_____

_____

_____

DAY 22

Remaining Connected to Our Purpose

Read Luke 19.

Focus: Luke 19:1-10

Reminding ourselves of our purpose as social workers is something we must do consistently. The beautiful story of Zacchaeus makes our calling worth all the challenges we face in our work. Like many of our clients, Zacchaeus made poor choices and needed the love of God just as our clients do. Because Jesus was clear about His purpose as the ultimate social worker, we see in verse 10 that He was able to meet Zacchaeus' need with confidence: to seek him and to save him.

We must be just as confident as Jesus was when we assist our clients. This requires us to have a well-rounded understanding of their needs and the services available to meet those needs. We may use various counseling techniques or draw on other skills and resources from other supportive services. Whichever way the Lord leads us, we must act with the assurance that comes from knowing our objective as social workers.

One of the reasons Jesus had such a positive effect on Zacchaeus is He was firmly connected to His main objective (see verse 10). We, therefore, see the impact such a connection can have on our clients. Are you firmly connected to your objective as a social worker? How can you strengthen that bond?

_____
_____
_____
_____
_____
_____
_____
_____
_____
_____
_____
_____
_____
_____
_____
_____
_____
_____
_____
_____
_____
_____
_____
_____
_____
_____

DAY 23

⤜❦❦❦⤏

"Let Go and Let God": Not Just a Cliché in Social Work

Read Luke 19.

Focus: Luke 19:41-44

In today's reading, again we see Jesus weeping for Jerusalem, a holy place where God's presence is felt and cherished. At the time of Jesus' work as the ultimate social worker, Jerusalem was spiritually desolate. Jesus' heart was so filled with sadness that He wept because of its present condition and its dark future.

There will be clients on our caseload that will go the way of Jerusalem. They will be determined to go their own way, even when it is unwise and dangerous. It is natural for us to have compassion and to mourn them; however, when it is clear that they will end up paying the consequences for their actions and ending up in ruins, we must not interfere with the events that will follow. We must allow God to use the situation to teach our clients what He wants them to learn. We can pray for them and support them in this process, but ultimately, we must do as Jesus did: accept their fate.

Recall a time when you wanted to help a client whose heart was not open to receive your assistance. How did you feel? Were you able to let the client go their way without intervening? Why or why not?

_____

_____

_____

_____

_____

_____

_____

_____

_____

_____

_____

_____

_____

_____

_____

_____

_____

_____

_____

_____

_____

_____

_____

_____

_____

_____

_____

DAY 24

Redirecting Questions: An Empowering Tool For Social Workers

Read Luke 20.

Focus: Luke 20:27-40

Our clients ask us such questions as, "What should I do?" "What do you think?" or "Why do you think he/she would do such a thing?" In these situations, it is not our job to provide our clients with answers but to ask them questions.

Today's reading shows the Jewish leaders trying to trap Jesus by asking Him a question that would cause Him to be arrested. Jesus, however, responded by posing a redirecting question that made them think carefully, not only about the question, but also about the consequences of their answer. They ultimately decided not to answer the question, leaving their original efforts to trap Jesus unsuccessful. By redirecting their question, therefore, Jesus accomplished two things: 1) He made them think deeply and prompted a discussion, and 2) He kept Himself from being trapped.

Our clients may not be attempting to trap us, but they will be expecting us to answer various questions that pertain to their lives, and we must help them find the answers to those questions. This empowers and assists them in working through their own challenges. Redirecting questions is a tool that opens the door to our clients' minds and allows them to see the answers are within themselves.

Are you answering questions from your clients? If so, why? If you are using redirecting questions, how can you refine this useful tool? Write a prayer asking God to show you the importance of redirecting questions and to assist you in mastering this wonderful art.

_____

_____

_____

_____

_____

_____

_____

_____

_____

_____

_____

_____

_____

_____

_____

_____

_____

_____

_____

_____

_____

_____

_____

_____

_____

_____

_____

_____

_____

DAY 25

Understanding Signs

Read Luke 21.

Focus: Luke 21:5-38

In today's reading, Jesus gives a vivid picture of the many signs of the end of the world. During our lives as Christians, we must recognize, understand, and take these signs seriously, and pray for wisdom each day to know how to interpret them.

Likewise, understanding signs such as culture, situations, body language, patterns, and behaviors is an important skill in the field of social work. We call such signs "triggers." As we work with our clients, we must be able to recognize triggers that prevent them from enjoying the beauty of emotional health.

Our job is to help our clients identify outside triggers that may lead to poor decision-making, unhealthy relationships, and ungodly thinking. As our clients become aware of these triggers, they can work on alternative ways of dealing with the situations that cause the triggers. Once they are able to accomplish this, we as social workers can assist our clients in exploring a healthier outlook on life.

Are you aware of the various triggers in your own life? Can you identify the triggers in the lives of your clients? If not, how can you begin to learn what triggers negative reactions in yourself and in your clients? Create a heartfelt prayer asking God to show you the importance of understanding signs and triggers in your life and in your clients' lives.

_____
_____
_____
_____
_____
_____
_____
_____
_____
_____
_____
_____
_____
_____
_____
_____
_____
_____
_____
_____
_____
_____
_____
_____
_____
_____
_____

DAY 26

Serving, The Foundation of Social Work

Read Luke 22.

Focus: Luke 22:24-30

In today's reading, Jesus is preparing His apostles for His departure. As He partakes with them in the Last Supper, He shares a beautiful example of His role on earth as the ultimate social worker. In the above verses, He describes Himself as a servant and encourages His disciples to see themselves as servants as well.

This humble view of ourselves is the foundation for our social work. We are to see ourselves as servants to our clients. We are to show them the same respect we would show to someone great, powerful, and influential, even though they may be poor, homeless, addicted to drugs, pregnant teens, or mentally ill. We have observed Jesus doing this throughout His earthly ministry. More importantly, we have seen Jesus' service to us in our own lives.

How do you see your clients? How can you elevate your view of them and humble your view of yourself in relation to them?

_____

_____

_____

_____

_____

_____

_____

_____

_____

_____

_____

_____

_____

Write a prayer asking the Lord to assist you in seeing yourself as a servant to your clients. Then ask God to give you creative ways to serve your clients.

_____

_____

_____

_____

_____

_____

_____

_____

_____

_____

_____

_____

_____

DAY 27

✦✦✦✦✦

Intercessory Prayer Born From
Knowledge of Our Clients

Read Luke 22.

Focus: Luke 22:31-32

We are all like the Apostle Peter in many ways. We can be abrasive, quick-tempered, and impulsive. In Peter, we see the elements of ourselves that we must give over to the Lord. Of course, Jesus knew all these things about Peter and had prayed for him, as per today's reading.

Knowing the various elements of our clients' characters is an important part of our job as social workers. Jesus, the ultimate social worker, shows us the benefits of knowing our clients well. Note how His knowledge of Peter prompted Him to intercede for him. Likewise, Jesus knows we will stumble, fall, and make poor choices. Because of this knowledge, He intercedes for us as He did for Peter, and as we must do the same for our clients

We must have the same love, compassion, and patience with our clients that Jesus demonstrated with Peter. We must not be surprised if our clients relapse, break the law, or have "meltdowns" because Satan desires to sift them like wheat. Instead use the knowledge of these possibilities to intercede for them so their faith does not fail. Then, after they repent, they can strengthen others like themselves.

How well do you know your clients? Do you intercede for them regularly? Why or why not? Create a prayer for your clients in the space below. Focus on their areas of weakness. Pray they develop a strong foundation of faith in the Lord and that this faith does not fail them.

_____

_____

_____

_____

_____

_____

_____

_____

_____

_____

_____

_____

_____

_____

_____

_____

_____

_____

_____

_____

_____

_____

_____

_____

_____

_____

_____

_____

_____

_____

_____

_____

DAY 28

Personal Maturity, A Requirement for Being a Social Worker

Read Luke 22.

Focus: Luke 22:49-51

Even though we are social workers, we are also human beings. This means we have personal struggles and challenges of our own. Many times, it is difficult to focus on our work with our clients due to private stressors in our own lives. This is where the maturity of being a social worker is seen.

In today's reading, we see Jesus under a tremendous amount of stress. He has just come from a trying time in prayer and now He is being arrested. His disciples are anxious and ready to fight. In all this confusion, the ear of the high priest's servant is cut off. And at the heart of this situation, Jesus heals him.

Jesus kept His focus on His work regardless of His inner turmoil. This level of personal maturity is required in our work. It comes from praying, as Jesus did before His arrest. It comes from loving our clients, as Jesus demonstrates throughout the book of Luke. It comes from keeping our hearts and minds on our goal, as Jesus did until His work was finished.

Prayerfully look into your heart and ask yourself how your personal challenges affect your social work. Do you allow the stress from your personal life to "spill over" into the way you serve your clients? How can you mature in this area of your professional life? Compose a prayer asking God to show you ways you can focus on your clients regardless of your own struggles.

_____
_____
_____
_____
_____
_____
_____
_____
_____
_____
_____
_____
_____
_____
_____
_____
_____
_____
_____
_____
_____
_____
_____
_____
_____
_____
_____
_____
_____

DAY 29

The Beauty of Forgiveness

Read Luke 23.

Focus: Luke 23:26-43

Forgiveness. We all are acquainted with that word. Some of us give it freely and others withhold it. In today's reading, we see Jesus giving it and asking God to give it as Jesus dies on the cross. He can forgive the scoffers and mockers because He understood they were not fully aware of the gravity of what they were doing.

Many of our clients also experience this lack of awareness. When they find themselves in difficult situations because they did not fully understand the consequences of their actions, they suffer from shame and guilt and are unable to move forward. They have a difficult time forgiving themselves because of things they may have done while intoxicated or angry.

The inability of our clients to forgive themselves can prevent growth in many areas of their lives. In such cases, a social worker's job is to educate our clients about the freedom that self-forgiveness brings. Jesus forgave those who did not appreciate the beautiful gift of love He was displaying by allowing Himself to be crucified. He understood they knew not what they did. This is an excellent lesson for social workers to use to assist our clients in forgiving themselves.

How can you use Jesus' example of forgiveness on the cross as a learning tool to assist your clients with this virtue?

_____

_____

_____

_____

_____

_____

_____

_____

_____

_____

_____

_____

_____

What obstacles do you anticipate will prevent you from showing the beauty and the freedom that comes with forgiveness? How can you overcome these obstacles for the benefit of your clients?

_____

_____

_____

_____

_____

_____

_____

_____

_____

_____

_____

_____

_____

DAY 30

Social Workers: Restorers of Hope

Read Luke 24.

Focus: Luke 24:13-34

Jesus has risen from the dead! In today's reading, we see Him walking with two of His followers, who were depressed because of Jesus' trial and crucifixion. They truly believed Jesus was the Messiah, and since they knew He died on the cross, their hope for a life of peace and oneness with God was gone. But note how Jesus guided them gently to the truth. God did not allow them to recognize Him initially, but by guiding them through the Scriptures that gave meaning to the events that had recently transpired they were eventually able to recognize Him. Seeing Him restored their hope.

This is the way we as social workers must work with our clients. When they no longer see the beauty in life and love, we must gently remind them of reasons to hope and live. We can do this by guiding them to recall triumphs of their past, present joys in their lives, and goals they wish to accomplish. In doing this, we help them see the purpose of their lives. We help them restore their hope.

Recall a client who was depressed and unmotivated. How did you handle that client? What tools did you use to bring them out of depression? List three creative ways in which you could restore hope in that client in the future.

_____

_____

_____

_____

_____

_____

_____

_____

_____

_____

_____

_____

_____

_____

_____

_____

_____

_____

_____

_____

_____

_____

_____

_____

_____

_____

_____

_____

DAY 31

Ending the Therapeutic Relationship with Grace and Skill

Read Luke 24

Focus: Luke 24:35-53

In the above verses, we see Jesus completing His earthly ministry as the ultimate social worker. He gives a blessing to His followers before He ascends into Heaven, empowering them to live life to the glory of God and share the Gospel with others. Note the grace and skill in which He ended His time on earth.

As social workers, we will leave the lives of clients at some point. You may end the therapeutic relationship because the client has met the goals of the treatment plan. Or you may get promoted and be unable to see the client in your new job. Whatever reason we end our relationships with our clients, we need to do it with the grace and skill in which Jesus ended His earthly ministry. He blessed and empowered His followers, giving them the tools needed to live an abundant life and be a blessing to others.

Recall the manner in which you ended a relationship with a client. Did you bless them by speaking well of them? Did you encourage them to help others? Compose a prayer asking God to show you how to end the therapeutic relationship with the grace and skill we see Jesus demonstrating in today's reading.

_____

_____

_____

_____

_____

_____

_____

_____

_____

_____

_____

_____

_____

_____

_____

_____

_____

_____

_____

_____

_____

_____

_____

_____

_____

_____

_____

_____

About the Author

Dr. June Tyson resides in Brooklyn, New York, and has twenty years of experience in counseling those whose lives have been affected by drugs, death, HIV/AIDS, homelessness, and loss of various kinds. She is a Licensed Clinical Social Worker (LCSW-R) and a member of the Academy of Certified Social Workers (ACSW). She practices psychotherapy at Community Counseling and Mediation (CCM) in Brooklyn. She has a Master's degree in Social Work from Fordham University and a Ph.D in Human Services from Capella University. She is an adjunct professor who teaches classes in diversity, counseling, and life coaching in the Master's in Counseling Program and the Master's in Social Work Program at Liberty University, Indiana Wesleyan University, and Winthrop University.

She enjoys traveling as a missionary to Thailand, Mexico, and Haiti, and has taught English to students in these countries. Dr. Tyson is also part of a Global Heath Group with whom she travels, sharing social work techniques with doctors and nurses of various hospitals and universities in Nigeria and Haiti. She believes social workers should expand their horizons to reach the entire world, not simply our communities. They should stretch themselves by learning other languages, doing missionary work, traveling, and working with populations outside their comfort zones.

Dr. Tyson has served the Christian community by teaching and living the Scriptures for more than thirty years. She is devoted to the things of the Lord and is led by the Holy Spirit in her professional and private life. Dr. Tyson is always looking for ways to learn and grow, and she looks forward to learning and growing with you.

Printed in the USA
CPSIA information can be obtained
at www.ICGtesting.com
LVHW090230021123
762762LV00001B/49